Black and White

Written by Dorothy Avery • Illustrated by Andrew Plant

2

It is black and white.

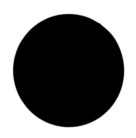

It eats grass.

4

It is a cow.

6

It is black and white.

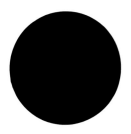

It eats insects and mice.

8

It is a skunk.

It is black and white.

It eats bamboo.

It is a panda.

It is black and white.

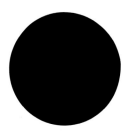

It eats fish.

16

It is a penguin.

18

It is black and white.

It eats seals.

It is a killer whale.

Zebras are black and white. They have stripes.

Black and white
can trick your eyes.

Index